DIGITAL AND INFORMATION LITERACY ™

CREATING MULTIMEDIA PRESENTATIONS

TAMRA B. ORR

rosen publishing's
rosen
central®

New York

*As always, to my children, who understand multimedia
much better than their mother*

Published in 2010 by The Rosen Publishing Group, Inc.
29 East 21st Street, New York, NY 10010

Library of Congress Cataloging-in-Publication Data

Orr, Tamra.
Creating multimedia presentations / Tamra B. Orr.—1st ed.
    p. cm.—(Digital and information literacy)
Includes bibliographical references and index.
ISBN-13: 978-1-4358-5319-5 (library binding)
1. Multimedia systems. 2. Presentation graphics software. I. Title.
QA76.575.O776 2010
005.5'8—dc22

                                                                    2008054736

Manufactured in the United States of America

CPSIA Compliance Information: Batch #WR014080YA For Further Information contact Rosen Publishing, New York, New York at 1-800-237-9932

CONTENTS

INTRODUCTION

Computers have changed everything from how you keep in touch with your friends to how you do your homework—and countless things in between. Whether you go online at school or at home or both, you are already aware of how large a role computers and the Internet play in your education. They help you perform your research and write your essays, and keep you connected with your teachers and other students in your class. In many ways, computers and the Internet can also help you create fantastic multimedia presentations for your next report, research paper, speech, or other class project.

Creating an interesting, fun, and successful presentation for one of your classes used to mean that you needed to break out the permanent markers and construction paper. Along with a ruler, some scissors, and a bottle of glue, you might have created a poster or a chart.

Today, you can still do that, of course, but your choices have expanded far beyond those simple supplies. By using multimedia, including downloaded photos, sounds, and video, you can add many different elements to your presentations. Going online and exploring the Internet can help you create projects that include text, charts, graphs, maps, photos, images, animation, music, video, audio, and more. Each one of these media sources can transform a flat, boring report into a dynamic and exciting one without

Cell phone calls, text messaging, and e-mailing photos are just some of the ways that our modern high-tech culture has come to depend on electronics for communication.

a great deal of extra work. Your choices do not end with the Internet, however. Many computers have their own built-in programs, such as PowerPoint, that can help you put together amazing reports that will wow your classmates and impress your teacher.

The suggestions, tips, and advice in this book will help you explore different types of multimedia to use in order to help spice up your presentation. They will guide you in what to do and not to do and what options to consider, as well as what effect each technique has on your presentation. What this book will not do, however, is act like a tutorial, with detailed steps describing precisely how to use PowerPoint, Corel Presentation, and other similar programs. The reasons for this are simple: these tutorials are changed and updated regularly, and the directions for each one depends entirely on what kind of computer you have and what programs are loaded onto it. This book does, however, include the links and information you need to find those tutorials when you are ready for them.

Putting together a multimedia presentation that shows how much you've learned, entertains your classmates, and pleases your teacher is easier than you'd think and more fun than you'd expect. Start experimenting and exploring, and see what you can create!

Chapter 1

Setting the Stage

Not all presentations call for fast, flashy animation or perky background music. Some are simple enough that only a few basic types of multimedia are needed to highlight and enhance your project's main points. Don't fall into the trap of thinking that if you throw in enough splash and color, it will turn a badly researched, sloppily constructed and organized, or content-poor project into a good one.

In that sense, presentations are a lot like Hollywood movies: special effects are nice and even thrilling to watch, but if the story is weak or confusing, or the acting is terrible, those special effects are not enough to rescue the film. The best clip art or most powerful audio or video clips cannot save your project if you haven't laid the necessary groundwork first.

Before you begin constructing a flip chart or going online to find the best Web site for creating bar graphs, you need to spend time on the very basics of your presentation. Start by imagining that you will not have anything to feature other than your text, or what you plan to write and/or say. Your words and the information they convey are the foundation of your

Although writing by hand has not completely disappeared from homework, pens, pencils, and paper have been steadily replaced by keyboards and computer monitors.

presentation. Just like with anything else you build, without a strong, dependable foundation, nothing else is secure.

The First Step: The Outline

The first step to creating a multimedia presentation is the same as it is for creating any other project: prepare a detailed outline. Put each one of your main points in the exact order in which you want to present them, including all of the relevant subpoints. This usually takes a few tries, so don't just do it once and assume it is good to go. Write it out, and then put it away for a while. After a day or two, come back to your outline. The time you spent away can easily make mistakes or necessary changes more obvious to you. Also, consider showing your outline to your parents, a friend, a teacher, or anyone who isn't as familiar with the topic as you are. They will be more likely to spot something confusing or missing from your outline.

Once you have all of your points and subpoints in the proper sequence, go back to the beginning and look at it from a new perspective. This time, search for places to include multimedia. Remember, look only for places where it will enhance the information you are presenting and is not thrown in as a way to make your presentation longer or appear more impressive. To determine if any kind of multimedia is actually valuable and worthwhile, ask yourself the following questions:

- Would a photograph or other illustration make this point easier to understand?
- Will the addition of a chart, graph, map, or diagram help explain any of my primary or secondary points?
- Would a video or audio clip support or illustrate a point I am trying to make?
- Will my audience have a better understanding of my topic with the addition of these multimedia elements?
- Will adding multimedia to my presentation help grab and hold my audience's attention?

Make sure your answer to each relevant question is yes before you decide to include some kind of multimedia. Otherwise, you may find that you are throwing these effects in simply to look tech savvy instead of in the interest of thoroughness. Your teacher will not appreciate this kind of "filler," which masks a lack of solid research and organization. Add multimedia because it improves your presentation, not because it's fun or slick. In other words, add it because it should be there, not just because it could be there.

The Second Step: Selecting and Placing Multimedia Elements

Once you have gone through your outline and pinpointed exactly where you want to include some form of multimedia, you need to figure out what type would fit best in each spot. Multimedia comes in many forms, from the ultra-simple to the relatively complex. Having a strong understanding of how to create each type of multimedia element and where it would fit best is the key to creating a multimedia presentation that is organized and effective.

Classroom multimedia choices include:

- Handouts
- Posters
- Flyers
- Bar graphs, line graphs, etc.
- Flowcharts, pie charts, flip charts, etc.
- Maps
- Diagrams
- Photographs
- Illustrations
- Clip art
- Slide presentations
- Animation
- Video clips
- Audio clips

Make a note within your outline precisely where you will place each type of media. You will spend the next hours, days, or weeks (depending on the size and complexity of your project) accommodating the enhancing multimedia effects you've chosen to the text (spoken or written words) of your presentation. When all the elements are in place, it is time to start practicing.

Whether preparing a book report, research paper, or classroom presentation, a growing number of students are turning to the computer and digital resources for brainstorming, organizing, drafting, and even presenting the project.

The Third Step: Practice, Practice, Practice

The old saying that "practice makes perfect" is quite true, especially when you are preparing a multimedia presentation. Some of your media will not necessarily affect the timing of your presentation (animation or clip art added to a slide, for example). Some media, however, such as handouts, slides, or video and audio clips, can alter the length and flow of your presentation. You need to know this ahead of time, especially if your teacher has set a strict time limit on your presentation.

Practicing a presentation in front of a mirror can teach you many important lessons about body language, facial expressions, gestures, posture, and style.

You will also need to practice so that you know how to smoothly incorporate your media into your speaking. If you have to pause to find your place in your script or notes every time after turning a page of your flip chart or pushing a key for the next PowerPoint slide, your presentation will probably sound choppy and go over its time limit. It is quite easy to completely lose your place and have to fumble around with your script until you find it again. This is embarrassing for you, frustrating for your audience (whose attention will begin to wander), and disruptive to your presentation.

Experts recommend that you practice out loud, from beginning to end, at least four times. At least one of those times should be in front of an audience so you can get helpful feedback. Not sure how you are doing? Have your friend or sibling grab a video camera and record your presentation. Watching it afterward may show you that some crucial piece of information is missing, that you say "uh" and "you know" far too many times, or that you are not making enough eye contact with your audience. You will also know how long each section takes and what kind of tinkering the multimedia requires in order to be presented smoothly and without malfunction. As the old saying goes, "If you fail to prepare, you are prepared to fail." Be prepared—to succeed!

A cautionary note: think ahead and have a plan B in place in case something happens to your multimedia. It might be something as simple as a frozen computer, a downed server, or a forgotten power cord or laptop battery that prevents you from retrieving and presenting computer- and Internet-based multimedia throughout your presentation. If you are not prepared to go through with your presentation without the multimedia enhancements, you may panic and your entire presentation will be blown. That is a much bigger problem than faulty electronics.

While your multimedia is there to help enhance and expand on your presentation, be prepared for the possibility that it could be lost in one way or another. This is when your words—that data that didn't require any special effects or tools other than your brain—can still shine through. The text of your presentation should be able to stand on its own, without the aid of multimedia enhancement, because it just may come to that!

MYTH You have to have a top-of-the-line, fully loaded home computer and high-speed Internet access to create a multimedia presentation.

FACT A number of the multimedia ideas in this book can actually be done by hand instead of on a computer and still look great. Computer access will give you more options, however, so if you can find one to use at home, a friend's house, school, or the public library, you may find you can be more creative, efficient, speedy, and productive. Most schools have computer labs and Internet access that will allow you to do the kind of computer-based work you want to do.

MYTH You have to be a computer geek to know how to use programs like PowerPoint.

FACT Most hardware and software programs have built-in tutorials that take you step-by-step through the process of generating multimedia elements for a presentation. There are hundreds of how-to books focusing on teaching the average person how to use a specific program, such as PowerPoint, Excel, Photoshop, or Illustrator.

MYTH All classroom presentations require a variety of multimedia.

FACT All presentations do not require multimedia. Ask your teacher what the multimedia requirements are for a project. If these components are necessary, your material and topic, as well as your own creativity, should determine how much and what kind to use.

Chapter 2

Charting Your Course

Even though technology continues to change the world on an almost daily basis, there is still a lot to be said for the old-fashioned methods of creating multimedia. Sitting at a table surrounded by poster board, permanent markers, and a couple of rulers is still an acceptable way to create many different types of graphics. You can design charts and graphs, transfer maps and diagrams, and make your own flip charts, handouts, and posters.

Of course, the Internet has made it much easier, faster, and simpler to do the same things on a computer. A number of sites can be found online that allow you to create clear and effective graphics. Just go to Google and type in "create _____" and you will be directed to a number of free download sites. Be aware, however, that some "free" downloads come bundled with malware, which can slow down a computer's performance, corrupt data, or compromise computer security. Ask a parent, teacher, or librarian to help you determine the safety of any programs you may want to download before you download them to your computer.

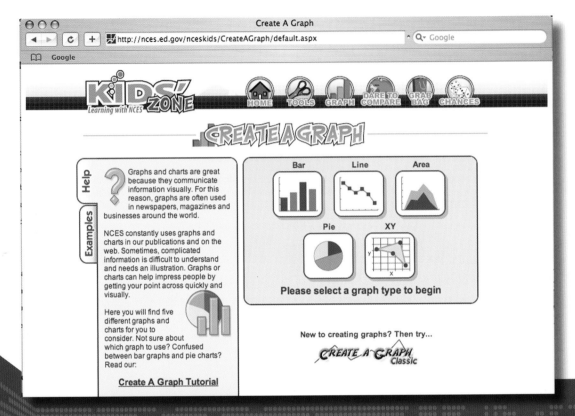

Kids' Zone (http://www.nces.ed.gov/nceskids/createAgraph) is a great site to go to learn how to create a variety of graphs and charts. It is easy to understand, and you can create different types of graphs to see which suits your data the best.

Graphs

One of the most reliable of these sites is Kids' Zone, sponsored by the National Center for Education Statistics (NCES). It can be found by visiting the NCES's Web site. Here you can find out all about creating bar, line, area, and other types of graphs. There is a built-in tutorial for additional help. Other sites help you create a graph or chart using Microsoft Excel.

Graphs, like most of the multimedia elements discussed in this book, are designed to help your audience understand material better. While auditory

Sites like Macworld (http://www.macworld.com) can show you new tricks and techniques for creating graphics that will enhance your project and make your data clear and easy to understand.

learners (those who learn best by listening) might comprehend your material best by hearing you speak, visual learners (those who learn best by seeing) will relate more to the graphics. In addition, complex concepts or statistics-heavy data are often easier to digest and comprehend if presented visually.

When generating bar graphs on a computer, you can easily select which way you want to lay out and orient the visual information—vertical (up and down) or horizontal (left to right). You can also easily choose what shape you want the images to be (rectangular is the most common). You can select colors, too. When color-coding different types of information and using more than one color, make sure that your colors are distinct from each other so there is no confusion. Below are two examples of bar graphs that you might create.

The first one is a vertical graph using rectangles that demonstrate how many books a student has read each summer over the past five years. The second one is a horizontal graph using different shapes (cylinders) and colors but representing the same information. Which one appeals to you the most? Why? Which one do you think conveys the information more clearly?

Below the two bar graphs is a line graph showing the same information yet again. How does the different format change the way you view, digest, and interpret the information?

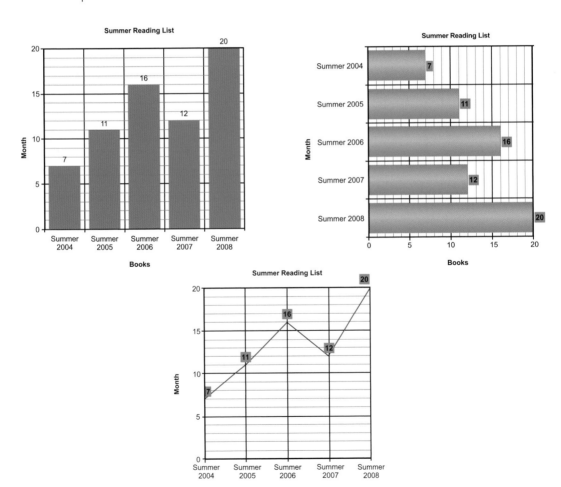

The following graph is called an area graph. This kind of graph shows trends, just as the bar graph does. What additional insight do you gain from the raw summer reading data when it's presented in this kind of visual format?

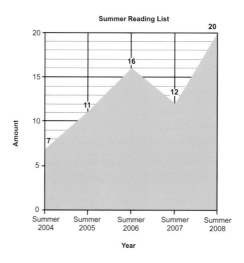

Another popular type of graph is the pie chart. Pie charts are most useful when you need to show how a large whole is being cut up into pieces of various sizes (hence the term "pie chart"). For example, if you want to show how your school's total budget was broken down between administrative and teacher salaries, student expenses, equipment costs, and classroom supplies, a pie chart would be the best way to present the data visually.

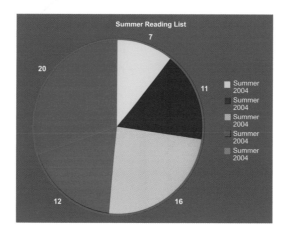

Charts and Diagrams

Depending on the content of your presentation, one of the types of charts you might want to include in your report is a flowchart. The technology to create one of these is in most Microsoft Office programs. Clicking on the drawing toolbar will lead you to most of the information you need. Click on "Autoshapes" to get started.

Flowcharts help you explain a process of some kind. They highlight the steps something must go through before successfully completing a task or a work cycle or reaching a typical outcome. A flowchart might detail how uranium found in rocks is transformed into the type used in nuclear weapons or the process of how you get up in the morning and get ready for school.

Another option to use is Venn diagrams, which are designed to show how two or more things are both alike and different. For example, if you were creating a Venn diagram about the *Harry Potter* and *The Lord of the Rings* series of books (written by J. K. Rowling and J. R. R. Tolkein, respectively), you would place unique information about each book in the outer edges of each of two overlapping circles. Plot elements, characters, types of creatures, locales, and authors would all be unique information that the two series of books don't share with each other (there are no Muggles or Voldemort in *Lord of the Rings* and no Hobbits or Gandalf in *Harry Potter*). They would be found in the outer part of each circle, where there is no overlap between the two spheres. In the middle, however, where the circles overlap, you would put elements that the two series of books have in common, such as "fantasy," "best-selling series," "movie adaptations," "magic," "fantastical creatures," "English authors," etc. You can have more than one set of circles if you are comparing multiple items, as in the diagram below.

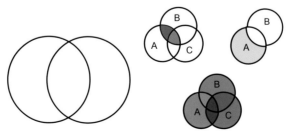

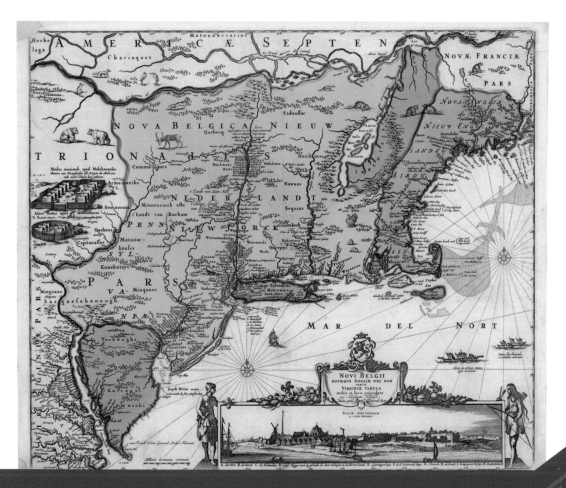

Maps are an excellent resource to add to your project. A vast variety of historical maps, such as this one of the early American colonies, are in the public domain and are available free from places like the Library of Congress (http://www.loc.gov).

Maps

Another element you might want to add to your presentation is a map. This is especially helpful when your topic has something to do with particular locations. It will help your audience understand what you are talking about and where it is located if they can see a relevant map. There are many

Local maps are simple to find online, such as this one of the Adams Morgan Heritage Trail from CulturalTourismDC.org. Along with checking out major search sites like Yahoo! and Google, you can also go to Mapquest or other driving direction sites and create maps by inputting street addresses.

different maps on the Internet that you can use. Simply put your search parameters into Google or another search engine and then hit "Maps" at the top of the selection page. You can also select "Images" to find more. Try to zero in on the areas that are most important to your presentation. If, for example, you are doing a presentation on an upcoming charity walk going on in your community, have a map that zooms in on the area encompassed by the walk route, not just a large map of your entire city.

Once you have created these graphs, charts, and other multimedia, the question is where to put them. You might be adding them to a handout, for example, that you want students to look at as you explain their significance. Or, you might add them to a flip chart that you have placed in the front of the room to go through, page by page, with your audience. You could also use one or more of the graphics on a poster or flyer. Others might be added to PowerPoint slides or other computer programs.

As you choose what kind of multimedia to use in your presentation, look at the examples shown here and figure out which one is best suited to the material you are trying to share. Double-check to make sure that every type of graphic you use is titled or labeled in some way so that your audience quickly understands the relevance of each one to the main idea, argument, or subject matter of your presentation. Remember that you want multimedia to make your project stronger, clearer, and more understandable—not more confusing!

TEN GREAT QUESTIONS

TO ASK A MULTIMEDIA LIBRARIAN

1. What kind of computer presentation program offers the best step-by-step, how-to tutorial?

2. Where should I look to make sure I am not violating any copyright laws?

3. How do I use a scanner to add my own photos or drawings to a report?

4. Where do I look for copyright-free video, audio, and image downloads?

5. How do I create my own video, audio, and image files to use in a presentation?

6. What equipment do I need to create homemade audio and video files?

7. What kind of digital camera takes the best pictures and is the easiest to use when downloading them to my computer? Is there a particular type of media card I should think about using?

8. What type of slide show program seems to be the easiest to understand and use?

9. Where can I go if I get stuck or don't understand something in the tutorial?

10. What seems to be the most useful or effective type of multimedia for an audience of fellow students?

Chapter 3

High-Tech Slide Shows

Slide shows have come a long way. No longer are they just someone else's boring pictures of places you've never been or a dry listing of a speech's main points. Today, thanks to computer programs, slide shows can be not only helpful and effective in conveying information but also colorful, musical, and even animated!

Helpful Resources and Tools

Many of today's computers come equipped with hardware that shows you just how to pull together an effective slide show. With Microsoft Office, that program is known as PowerPoint, and it can be used with both PCs and Macs. Other useful slide show programs include Apple Presentations, Apple's Keynote, Corel Presentations, Google Docs, and Kid Pix. These programs are so rich in resources that entire books have been devoted to showing readers how to make the best use of them. Trying to describe all of their individual features and how to access each of them is beyond the scope of this book. But rest assured that the tutorials that come with the programs are very clear and easy to follow.

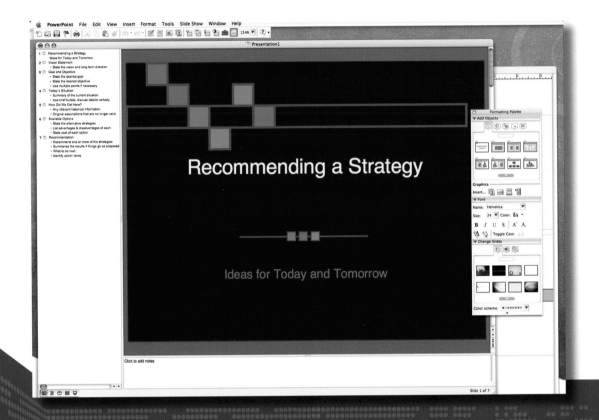

PowerPoint presentations are used everywhere from classrooms to executive boardrooms. They are perfect for highlighting your main points and illustrating your argument.

If you do get confused, just stop by the library and pick up one of the hundreds of how-to books written about each program. You could also speak to the library's multimedia or information technology expert for helpful tips. In addition, your school may offer after-school computer skills classes in which you can learn multimedia research and presentation techniques, among many other computer and Internet skills. Local community colleges and community centers also offer a wide variety of computer skills classes for the general population.

Regardless of what type of slide presentation you end up using, the rules about what to put and not put on those slides stay the same. As you

Copyright Law and Fair Use

Most printed and online materials have a copyright. A copyright is the legal right to publish and sell a work (including text, images, and audio and video recordings). If someone else wants to print, copy, or download the work, that person needs permission from the person or company that has the copyright. This copyright law helps protect the rights of the person who created the work.

However, as a student, you may not have to worry too much about asking for permission to use material from the Internet in your school reports. Most of the projects you do for school will fall under the category called fair use. The term "fair use" is part of the U.S. copyright law that says that material may be quoted exactly, without permission from the creator, as long as credit is given to the creator and the material used is reasonably short. Fair use applies to multimedia works as well as printed works.

go through the individual slide show program's tutorial and begin creating your own slide show, keep the following tips and advice in mind.

Styling

Fiddle around with different fonts. There are so many font choices on computers today that you're bound to find something that perfectly suits your presentation. Don't be tempted to use some of the wackier ones, such as Jokerman, Juice ITC, Neurochrome, Quigley Wiggly, or Westminster. Yes, they are fun and perfect for an e-mail to a friend on his or her birthday or for making a scrapbook page, but they are not appropriate for a

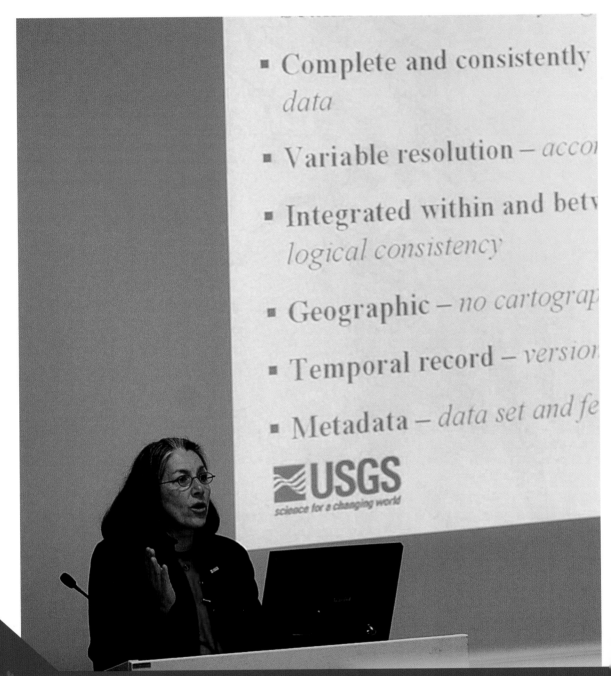

Using visual aids during your presentation can help ensure that both your auditory and your visual learners are absorbing the information.

classroom presentation where legibility is your number-one priority. The words have to be easily read, even for students sitting in the back of the classroom. And your font should echo the tone of your presentation—serious, professional, and clear. Stick to the usual ones: Times New Roman, Tahoma, Arial, or Franklin Gothic Book.

You will need to figure out what size font to use. Remember that you want the student in the very back row of the classroom to be able to read your slides without any effort. Often this means using a font size of 28 for most text, with titles appearing in 36. If you aren't sure, try different sizes and see if you can read them from across the room. For emphasis, you can use the **bold**, *italics* and <u>underlining</u> features. Use them only when they are needed—don't go overboard. They can lose their power if overused.

Almost every slide you write should have some kind of header or title. This helps your audience recognize the relevance of the information right away. If you have three or four slides that elaborate on a single item or topic, you do not need to continue the title on each one of those related slides. The first in the group of slides can contain the header. As soon as you go to another topic, however, you need a header indicating that you have now moved on to another topic within the presentation.

Most programs let you play around with background colors and text colors. As a general rule, if your background is dark, have lightly colored text and vice versa. Remember that this isn't art class—you aren't trying to play with tints and shades. You want your slides to be legible above all else. Limit the colors on a page. The use of too many colors and too many color shifts gets visually confusing. If you want to emphasize a word or phrase, you can make it a different color. But generally, stick to one color of text. Cleanness, clarity, and simplicity are the ideals.

Be Consistent

Once you have chosen your colors, font, and style, keep them consistent. Don't experiment with different combinations on other slides. The time for experimenting is when you are still making up your mind. By the time your audience sees your presentation, each slide should be uniform in appearance and design. There should be a unified look to your slide presentation. On the other hand, don't make each slide identical to the ones before and after it. It's a tricky balancing act, but one that you need to figure out. You want to add enough different kinds of graphics and variety of visual content that your audience doesn't get bored.

Keep It Simple

When you are deciding what to put on the slides, remember that they should only be the highlights or main points of what you are discussing. You want people to be listening to you and not reading the slides. Keep it concise and brief. Avoid long lines of words. As a rule, keep everything justified (aligned) to the left. But if you have a list, you can center it in the middle of the slide with bullet points (dots) before each item. As a rule, include no more than four bullet points per slide. Double-space between the lines. If you find yourself running out of room, you are saying too much on one slide and need to either edit or continue on to the next slide.

Photos, Illustrations, and Clip Art

Another way to add life and additional meaning to your presentation is through some kind of illustration. There are a number of ways to do this.

The quickest way to search online for images is to use a search engine like Google. In fact, Google has its own section just for searching for images. After reaching the Google homepage, click on the "Images" button. You will be brought to the Google page for searching for images only. Simply type into the search field the name of the image you wish to search for and Google will list the results. Picsearch is another search engine dedicated to finding photos online.

Become familiar with clip art, which is art that is copyright free, meaning you can use it in your presentation without having to pay for it. Clip art includes drawings, cartoons, icons, images, and photos that are yours to use

A number of Web sites are located throughout the Internet to help you understand how to add multimedia to your presentations. This one is called Presentation Helper (http://www.presentationhelper.co.uk). Glance through several to see what ideas they may inspire.

as you see fit. You can find them on the Internet in a number of places. Microsoft Office Online can guide you to thousands of royalty-free images and sounds. Classroom Clipart features alphabetical listings of clip art that can be used in the classroom. Also check out the clip art selection at School Clip Art. In addition, if you go to large bookstores like Barnes and Noble or Borders, you will find entire books of clip art that include CDs, so you can download the images directly into your presentation or store them on

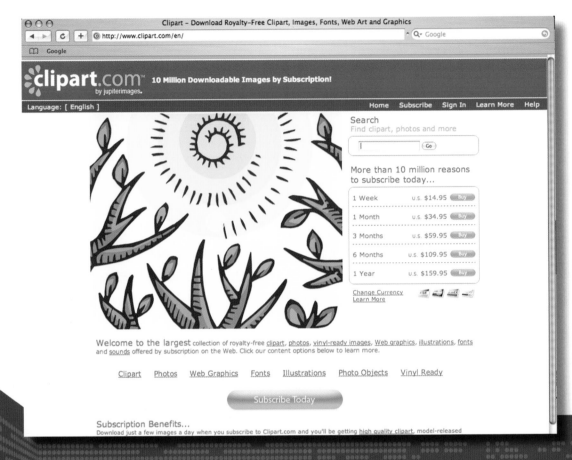

Sites like ClipArt.com can help you add any one of thousands of drawings and photographs to your presentation without having to worry about copyright infringement.

your computer. There are also many clip art collections available through Amazon.com.

One important collection of royalty-free images is available from the Library of Congress, which has an archive of hundreds of thousands of historic images available for free download. Other government and public organizations, such as the National Aeronautic and Space Administration (NASA), have large royalty-free photo collections.

A scanner can come in quite handy if you want to add your own artwork to your presentation. Scanners are also relatively easy to use.

Why can't you just go online and pick any image you want and include it in your report? It is the same reason why you just can't pick up a book and include the author's words as your own. Those words—and those images— belong to someone, and using them without permission is breaking copyright laws. You are using artists' property without their permission. It is akin to stealing because artists make their money by selling their work, not by giving it away.

You can, of course, avoid copyright complications by adding your own photos, drawings, and illustrations to your presentation. All you need is a scanner, which makes a digital copy of a text document, photo, or other image just as a photocopier makes a paper copy. The image can then be loaded into your computer and transferred to wherever you need it to be. But be sure to keep track of files and keep them organized. Create folders to store files in, and name them so you can easily locate them when your research is finished.

Adding photos, illustrations, pictures, and slides to your presentation can help your audience grasp the information better and enjoy the process more than they might have without the multimedia. It can also make the project more fun for you and teach you computer skills that you will very likely use many, many more times in the future.

Chapter 4

Sound and Vision

In addition to everything else they can do, PowerPoint and other multimedia programs also offer the ability to add video and audio clips to your presentations. Now you can show a short (experts recommend forty-five seconds or less) film related to your discussion or include an audio clip of a speech, interview, or report on your topic. You can even provide a soundtrack or sound effects to enhance and enliven your presentation.

Before you begin exploring the different options for adding audio and video clips, however, ask yourself the questions posed in the first chapter of this book. Make sure that these audiovisual additions will truly enhance your presentation and are not being added simply to fill up empty space, disguise a lack of research or writing, or impress everyone with your technical skills.

Finding Audio and Video Clips

To search for suitable video clips, use a general search engine. The two most popular methods for finding video today on the Internet are YouTube

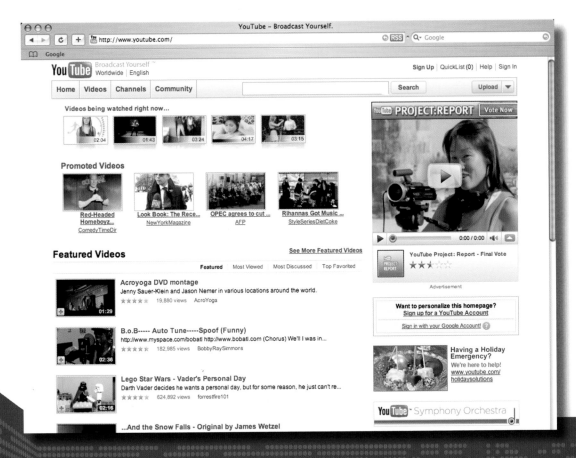

Almost any type of video image can be found on YouTube.com. By using the right words in the search box, you may find hundreds of videos to use.

and Google Video. Unlike specialized sites, however, YouTube and Google Video are likely to return thousands of videos for every keyword search you input. You will have to wade through a lot of irrelevant videos before you strike upon a worthwhile one. This is why it's better to search a site more closely tailored to your subject, such as National Geographic, PBS, Discovery, NOVA, the Library of Congress, NASA, CNN, or other news, documentary, and educational sites.

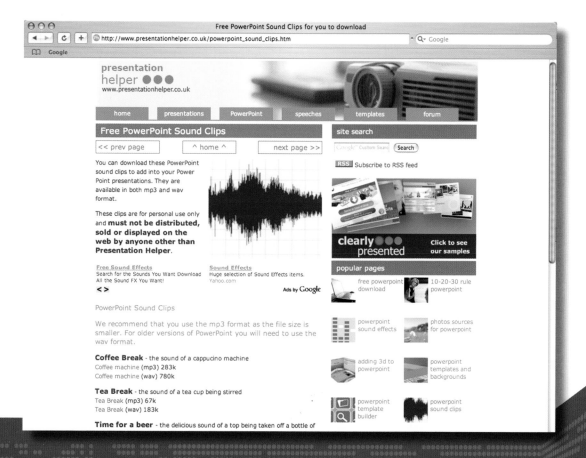

Many audio clips can be found online. Look at sites that offer presentation help, tips, and ideas to find them, such as Presentation Helper (http://www.presentationhelper.co.uk).

Audio clips, such as a portion of a speech, song, documentary, or news or interview program, or sound effects, can be added to your presentation as well. You can use search engines like Google to find audio clips to download. Some search engines are dedicated specifically to locating audio and video files. Such sites as AltaVista and Yahoo! Audio Search are among the most popular. Simply enter the sound, speech, or song you are looking for.

File   Edit   View   Favorites   Tools   Help

      MAKING THE GRADE

Making the Grade

How your multimedia project is graded will vary from one teacher to the next. One way to see how your project might measure up is to go online and look at some of the guidelines, or rubrics, set up for scoring this type of presentation. Just put "multimedia presentation rubric" in the search box. Here is what a standard multimedia presentation rubric might look like:

SKILLS	Excellent	Satisfactory	Needs Improvement
Organization/ Preparation	A clear introduction, body, and conclusion included; sequence is logical; easy to follow; clear sense of time spent in preparation.	A sense of organization is apparent; sequence is clear for the most part; time spent preparing is fairly clear	No clear sense of organization; no clear introduction or conclusion to support the main ideas; seems hurried
Writing/Subject Knowledge	All is well researched; shows clear understanding of major ideas; substantial research was performed	Some subject knowledge; with some errors or misunderstandings	Time spent researching is not evident; information is confusing or jumbled
Technical/ Navigation	Includes a variety of graphics; has a professional look; all graphics are relevant in topic; no technical glitches; easily navigates through different types of media; screens are easy to understand and read	Some graphics are used to highlight points; some are not quite necessary; a technical glitch here and there; familiarity navigating through the media; screens are helpful although sometimes crowded or confusing	Very little graphics, if any, or they are used inappropriately or thrown in for effect; repeated technical glitches; awkwardness with navigation; screens do not help but distract from the actual presentation
Grammar, Punctuation, Spelling	No spelling, punctuation, grammar, or usage errors to be found	Only one or two slight errors	A number of errors in all aspects
Originality/ Creativity	Inventive; not mimicking other reports	Creative; only a few references or similarities to other reports	Clear imitation of what has already been done on the topic

Keep the goals and requirements mentioned in this rubric in mind as you research and organize your presentation. This helps tailor it to your teacher's highest expectations.

Other places on the Internet to find audio clips are from major news organizations, library databases, collections, and archives. Web sites like the one belonging to the U.S. Library of Congress have archives of information that may not be found easily through a broader search engine. Free downloads are ideal, but remember that you must not violate any copyright laws. Downloading music or other copyrighted files off the Internet without paying for them is illegal, even for purposes of research. Luckily, there are many millions of audio files that are in the public domain or have been made freely available to the public.

Placing and Editing Your Clips

Slide show and multimedia presentation programs allow you to insert scanned images, clip art, charts, graphs, video and audio links, and other multimedia. The key to incorporating audio and video clips depends on what program you are using and what type of computer you have.

Within the computer's slide show program, you should see a place to insert a clip. For example, in PowerPoint, it is found under the "Insert" tab. Three-quarters of the way down the drop-down menu is "Movies and Sounds." It gives you several options to choose from. There is also specialized software that allows you to edit the clips you add to your presentation so that they can be pared down to the length that you want and the exact portion of the video or audio that you want. Windows Movie Maker is one example and is available for download at Microsoft's Web site.

Tutorials on how to incorporate video clips in PowerPoint presentations can be found online. Simply place a term like "video clips PowerPoint" in your search engine and visit some of the Web sites that turn up. For using Adobe to create your own videos and Flash animation, a tutorial be can found at Adobe's Web site. Different software packages can teach you how to download audio files. One example is Adobe Encore CS4, and information on it can be found at Adobe's Web site, Adobe.com.

A Fully Engaged Audience

One computer company's slogan states, "Tell me and I will forget. Show me and I will remember. Involve me and I will understand." For the student putting together a successful multimedia presentation, this is important advice. By involving your audience in your presentation—by encouraging them to listen, read, watch, and respond—you are helping your classmates learn. In the process, you are gaining valuable digital and information technology skills that will serve you well throughout your entire life.

audio clip A brief recording of sound (noise, music, words, etc.) added to a presentation.

clip art Copyright-free photos, drawings, and other illustrations that can be included in a presentation without payment or permission.

copyright The exclusive right to make copies, license, or use a literary, musical, or artistic work.

download To transfer and copy digital information from one computer to another.

fair use The part of U.S. copyright law that says material may be quoted exactly, without permission from the creator, as long as credit is given to the creator and the material used is reasonably short.

font A computer style of making letters and text; a style of appearance for letters and numbers when printed or shown on-screen.

Internet The virtual network connecting millions of computers worldwide.

multimedia The combined use of several media, or types of information delivery, such as sound, text, and video.

rubric A type of grading format that outlines standards at excellent, satisfactory, and unsatisfactory levels; a system of guidelines and criteria for evaluating and grading someone's work.

search engine A Web site that uses software designed to locate documents that exist on millions of computers connected to the Internet.

tutorial An online teaching tool, akin to a virtual one-on-one class or seminar, that instructs computer users how to do something new or how to use a new program.

video clip A brief segment of a movie, television show, home video, or other video recording that can be added to a multimedia presentation.

Computers for Youth
322 Eighth Avenue, Floor 12A
New York, NY 10001
(212) 563-7300
Web site: http://www.cfy.org
Computers for Youth provides inner-city students with home computers and
provides training, technical support, and online training so that they
can do better in school.

Copyright Kids
The Copyright Society of the U.S.A.
352 Seventh Avenue, Suite 739
New York, NY 10001
Web site: http://www.copyrightkids.org
Copyright Kids is a part of the Copyright Society of the U.S.A. It offers
information about copyrights of art, music, video, and other media
found online.

Get Net Wise
Internet Education Foundation
1634 I Street NW
Washington, DC 20009
Web site: http://www.getnetwise.org
Get Net Wise is part of the Internet Education Foundation, which works to
provide a safe online environment for children and families.

Just Think
39 Mesa Street, Suite 106
San Francisco, CA 94129

(415) 561-2900
Web site: http://justthink.org
Just Think is a nonprofit foundation that promotes media literacy for
    young people.

Media Awareness Network
1500 Merivale Road, 3rd Floor
Ottawa, ON K2E6Z5
Canada
(613) 224-7721
Web site: http://www.media-awareness.ca
The Media Awareness Network creates media literacy programs for
    young people. The site contains educational games about the
    Internet and media.

Web Sites

Due to the changing nature of Internet links, Rosen Publishing has developed
an online list of Web sites related to the subject of this book. This site is
updated regularly. Please use this link to access this list:

http://www.rosenlinks.com/dil/mult

FOR FURTHER READING

Bullard, Lisa. *Ace Your Oral or Multimedia Presentation*. Berkeley Heights, NJ: Enslow Publishers, 2009.

Fahs, Chad. *How to Do Everything with YouTube*. New York, NY: The McGraw-Hill Companies, 2008.

Furgang, Adam. *Searching Online for Image, Audio, and Video Files* (Digital and Information Literacy). New York, NY: Rosen Publishing, 2010.

Gaines, Ann. *Ace Your Internet Research* (Ace It! Information Literacy). Berkeley Heights, NJ: Enslow Publishers, 2009.

Hawthorn, Kate. *A Young Person's Guide to the Internet*. New York, NY: Routledge, 2005.

Lowe, Doug. *PowerPoint 2007 for Dummies*. Hoboken, NJ: For Dummies, 2006.

McGraw-Hill/Irwin. *Multimedia Presentation Skills, Student Edition* (Professional Communication). New York, NY: Career Education, 2003.

Shaw, Maura D. *Mastering Online Research*. Cincinnati, OH: Writer's Digest Books, 2007.

Sorenson, Sharon. *A Quick Reference to Internet Research*. New York, NY: Amsco School Publishing, Inc., 2004.

Souter, Gerry, et al. *Bringing Photos, Music, and Video into Your Web Page*. Berkeley Heights, NJ: Enslow Publishers, 2003.

Taylor, Allan, et al. *Career Opportunities in the Internet, Video Games, and Multimedia*. New York, NY: Checkmark Books, 2007.

Walker, Janice R., and Todd Taylor. *The Columbia Guide to Online Style*. New York, NY: Columbia University Press, 2006.

Willard, Nancy E. *Cyber-Safe Kids, Cyber-Savvy Teens: Helping Young People Learn to Use the Internet Safely and Responsibly*. Hoboken, NJ: Jossey-Bass, 2007.

BIBLIOGRAPHY

Atkinson, Cliff. *Beyond Bullet Points: Using Microsoft Office PowerPoint 2007 to Create Presentations That Inform, Motivate, and Inspire.* Redmond, WA: Microsoft Press, 2008.

Duarte, Nancy. *Slideology: The Art and Science of Creating Presentations.* Sebastopol, CA: O'Reilly Media, Inc., 2008.

Finkelstein, Ellen. *PowerPoint for Teachers: Dynamic Presentations and Interactive Classroom Projects.* Hoboken, NJ: Jossey-Bass, 2007.

Joss, Molley. *Looking Good in Presentations.* Scottsdale, AZ: Coriolis Group Books, 1999.

Lake, Susan. *Multimedia and Image Management.* Boston, MA: South-Western Educational Publishing, 2005.

Lehman, Carol M. *Creating Dynamic Multimedia Presentations: Using Microsoft PowerPoint.* Boston, MA: South-Western College Publishing, 2003.

Moran, Barbara. *Crafting Multimedia Text: Websites and Presentations.* Upper Saddle River, NJ: Prentice Hall, 2004.

Weir, Kathie. *School Projects, Papers, and Presentations.* Los Angeles, CA: Parent's Guide Press, 2002.

Wempen, Faithe. *PowerPoint Advanced Presentation Techniques.* Hoboken, NJ: Wiley, 2004.

INDEX

About the Author

Tamra B. Orr is the author of numerous nonfiction books for readers of all ages. She has won several awards for her books, but praise from her kids is her personal favorite accolade. She is an avid reader and an old-fashioned letter writer, but she is also extremely tech-savvy. Yet, she admits that whenever she is creating any kind of multimedia presentation, she will occasionally seek the advice and know-how of her youngest—and most cyber-literate— child. She and her husband live in the Pacific Northwest with one dog, one cat, and four kids (ages twelve to twenty-four).

Photo Credits

Cover, p. 1 (left) © www.istockphoto.com/Stephen Krow; cover, p. 1 (second from right), p. 8 © www.istockphoto.com/Leslie Banks; cover, p. 1 (right) www.istockphoto.com/Matjaz Boncina; p. 5 © www.istockphoto.com/ Rich Legg; p. 11 © Shutterstock; p. 12 © Sjkold/The Image Works; p. 21 Library of Congress Maps Division; p. 28 © Stephen D. Cannerelli/The Image Works; p. 33 © Michael Newman/Photo Edit.

Designer: Nicole Russo; Photo Researcher: Marty Levick